LINKING THE PAST AND PRESENT

WHAT DID THE
ANCIENT
ROMANS
DO FOR ME?

Patrick Catel

D1324030

Raintree

www.raintreepublishers.co.uk

Visit our website to find out more information about Raintree books.

To order:

☎ Phone 0845 6044371

▤ Fax +44 (0) 1865 312263

▧ Email myorders@raintreepublishers.co.uk

Customers from outside the UK please telephone +44 1865 312262

Raintree is an imprint of Capstone Global Library Limited, a company incorporated in England and Wales having its registered office at 7 Pilgrim Street, London, EC4V 6LB - Registered company number: 6695582

Edited by Megan Cotugno and Laura Knowles
Designed by Richard Parker
Original illustrations © Capstone Global Library Limited 2010
Illustrated by Roger@KJA-artists.com
Picture research by Hannah Taylor
Originated by Capstone Global Library Limited
Printed and bound in China by CTPS

ISBN 978 0 431 082 57 8 (hardback)
14 13 12 11 10
10 9 8 7 6 5 4 3 2 1

ISBN 978 1 406 25882 0 (paperback)
15 14 13 12
10 9 8 7 6 5 4 3 2 1

British Library Cataloguing in Publication Data
Catel, Patrick.
What did the ancient Romans do for me?. -- (Linking the past and present)
937-dc22
A full catalogue record for this book is available from the British Library.

Acknowledgements

We would like to thank the following for permission to reproduce photographs: Alamy Images pp. **9** (imagebroker), **15** (© Bill Lyons); Corbis pp. **11** (epa/ M.A. Pushpa Kumara), **17** (Reuters/Kim Kyung-Hoon), **19** (Xinhua Press/ Chen Xie); istockphoto pp. **7** (© S. Greg Panosian), **12**, **13** (© gaffera), **27** (©Marco Maccarini); Photolibrary pp. **21** (Victor Kotler), **23** (Michael Jaeger); shutterstock p. **25** (© bsankow).

Cover photograph of the Pont du Gard Bridge in Roussillon, Languedoc, France reproduced with permission of Photolibrary/Medio Images.

We would like to thank Dr Ray Laurence for his invaluable help in the preparation of this book.

Every effort has been made to contact copyright holders of material reproduced in this book. Any omissions will be rectified in subsequent printings if notice is given to the publisher.

All the Internet addresses (URLs) given in this book were valid at the time of going to press. However, due to the dynamic nature of the Internet, some addresses may have changed, or sites may have changed or ceased to exist since publication. While the author and publisher regret any inconvenience this may cause readers, no responsibility for any such changes can be accepted by either the author or the publisher.

Contents

Look for the Then and Now boxes. They highlight parts of ancient Roman culture that are present in our modern world.

Any words appearing in the text in bold, **like this**, are explained in the glossary.

What did the ancient Romans do for me?

When you put your socks on in the morning, do you stop to think of who invented them? When you set your alarm for a.m. or p.m., do you ever wonder where those letters came from? When you and your family hop in a car or on to a bus, you probably take the smooth road under you for granted. Perhaps you have a favourite book to read on the way?

You can thank the Romans for all of these ideas. Many words and phrases that we use, such as a.m. and p.m., come from Latin, the Roman language. The Romans made excellent roads that crossed their **empire**, very much like the motorways of today. They also invented the **codex**, which is similar to our modern book. The Romans even invented socks! There are many other Roman ideas and inventions that we still use today.

Gladiator fights were a popular type of entertainment in ancient Rome.

Thousands of people went to the Colosseum in Rome to watch gladiator fights and other games. Does the Colosseum remind you of a type of building we still use today?

Who were the Romans?

Legend says that Rome was founded by Romulus in 753 BC, after he killed his brother Remus. In this story, Romulus and Remus were the twin sons of Mars, the god of war. In fact, Rome began as a village built on seven hills by the River Tiber, in what is now Italy. The hills were useful for defence, because the Romans could see their enemies coming from far away. The river provided water for farming and made travelling to the sea very easy.

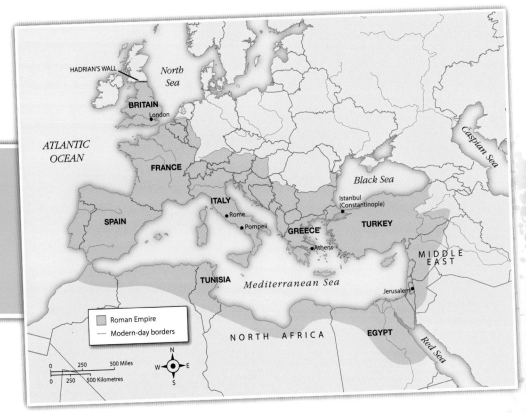

This map shows the Roman Empire when it was strongest, around AD 101–107.

The Roman Republic was formed in 509 BC and lasted until 27 BC. The Roman **Empire** followed, lasting from 27 BC to AD 476. Over time, the empire grew to include lands all over Europe, North Africa, and the Middle East. The Romans defended this empire with one of the mightiest armies in history.

The Romans were influenced by ancient Greek culture. They copied many ancient Greek customs, even taking on some of their gods. Roman art and sculpture were also copied from ancient Greek originals. However, the Romans did make their own mark on history. They took on massive building projects, such as **aqueducts**, sewer systems, **amphitheatres** (stadiums), and bridges. Many of these still survive today and are as impressive as any of our modern structures. The Romans also influenced the way we make laws and organize governments today.

The Colosseum in Rome was the largest amphitheatre in the Roman Empire. It could hold up to 50,000 people!

Roman nicknames

Nicknames were common in ancient Rome, and they weren't always nice. The nickname Brutus, for example, meant dimwit!

What was daily life like for the Romans?

The Romans enjoyed sports such as wrestling, running, weightlifting, and boxing. They also kept dogs, cats, birds, and fish as pets. Girls played with dolls made from cloth, bone, or clay. Boys and girls played hide-and-seek and marbles. Adults enjoyed a board game called Robbers, which was similar to chess.

Public baths

The Romans thought keeping clean was important, and built many public baths. Men and women bathed at different times and often used the baths as a place to meet friends, to exercise, and even to read. Bathing was very different then. For example, the Romans didn't have soap. They rubbed oil on to their body, then scraped it off with a **strigil**, which was a piece of curved metal.

Roman detergent

The Romans washed clothes in a cleaning solution to keep them white. One of the ingredients of the solution was urine (wee)! The clothes came out clean in the end, though.

THEN...

The Romans **worshipped** gods and held festivals. They also had **superstitions**. A superstition is a fear of the unknown or mysterious that is not based on reason or knowledge. The Romans believed in curses and charms. People even hired a professional curse writer if they were really angry at someone! Roman children were given a bulla at birth. This was like a locket they wore around their necks for protection against evil.

These ruins of Roman public toilets were found near Rome, Italy. Romans used a shared sponge on a stick instead of toilet tissue!

...NOW

Today, people often still keep lucky charms. Other Roman customs stayed with us as well. Many of today's wedding customs can be traced to ancient Roman times. This includes wearing a ring on the fourth finger, as well as serving a wedding cake to guests. The ancient Romans offered wine to the gods to bless new ships and their crews. Today, we break a bottle of wine on the front of a new ship to bring it good luck. Many modern holidays began as ancient Roman festivals, or took on similar customs.

Food and drink

The Romans ate many foods that we can recognize today, such as bread, fruits, vegetables, fish, and chicken. However, they also liked ostrich brains, eel-like fish called lampreys, and a small rodent called a dormouse. Poor people could only afford meat on special occasions. The wealthy, on the other hand, ate pearls, and sometimes sprinkled gold on top of vegetables!

Here, a Roman man is shown wearing a white tunic with a coloured cloak. His cloak is pinned with a metal brooch.

THEN...

The Romans used their clothes as a way to look good, but also to show how wealthy they were. Most Roman men wore white **tunics** or **togas**. Togas were 6 metres (20 feet) long and were wrapped loosely around the body. The emperor and his officials often wore purple. Women from rich families wore make-up and jewellery.

The ancient Romans drank water that was collected when it rained or was brought in to the city by **aqueducts**. They also drank wine and other drinks mixed with honey. They used roses in wine and pies. "Fast-food" stalls in the city sold things like fish, sausages, chicken, bread, and wine.

Modern armies use uniforms and marks of rank influenced by the Romans. You can tell that Sri Lanka's army commander (right) is very important from his uniform.

Sandals and socks?

Most Romans wore sandals. The Romans also invented socks, which we can all appreciate on a cold day!

...NOW

People still use their clothes to display their wealth and social position. They buy jewellery and clothes from designer labels. Business people and politicians wear suits. Different jobs, such as the police, the army, and fire fighters, have their own uniforms.

How was Roman society organized?

Roman society was not equal. The **plebeians**, who were the ordinary, working people, had few rights. Neither did women, who were expected to keep the house and raise children. There were also many slaves in Rome. Slaves could sometimes buy back their freedom. They could even become citizens. However, they could also be beaten or killed by their masters.

The Romans made metal coins from brass, bronze, gold, and silver. They were stamped with pictures of gods and the ruling emperor.

THEN...

In order to help them keep order over their large empire, the Romans took a census, which is a count, of the population. They also made sure that the same coins and systems of weights and measures were used all over the empire. In this way, they knew that trade would be fair to everyone, no matter where in the empire they lived.

Roman classes

Wealthy Romans were called **patricians**. They sometimes had hundreds of slaves. Slaves were brought to Rome from all over the **empire**. Some were highly educated and tutored their master's children. The patricians respected teachers, whatever class they came from. Plebeian workers who were not slaves included merchants and craftsmen, who sold goods and food at stands in the city. Some craftsmen were wealthy and became famous for their works.

The euro is used in many European countries today, much as Roman coins were used across the empire.

The Roman census

One of the reasons the Romans took a census was to know which men qualified for military service. Many modern countries do the same.

...NOW

Today, most countries take a census of their population. This helps them plan such things as how many schools, hospitals, and roads need to be built. We also have international rates of exchange, which means that we can work out how much our money is worth in another country. There are also agreed forms of measurements used everywhere.

How did the Romans keep law and order?

A Roman document known as the **Justinian Code** contained hundreds of comments on the law. The ancient Romans used ideas of **impartial** justice and a **jury** trial. These ideas influenced modern law in Europe and the United States.

Legal rights

As in most countries today, citizens of Rome had certain legal rights. One was the right of due process. This means that laws must be stated clearly and carried out fairly. Roman citizens had the right to defend themselves and be tried by a jury. They could also **appeal** a court's decision and try to get it changed. Slaves didn't have these rights, and the rich often received special treatment. Roman punishments were harsh.

Ancient graffiti

Graffiti was common in Roman cities. One example from ancient times was "Helena amatur ab Rufo", which means "Rufus Loves Helen". Another, inside a school, said "Socrates taedium est", which means "Socrates is boring"!

THEN...

One of the ways in which the Romans were able to keep order and peace in their **empire** was by being open to other cultures. As the empire grew, it took on some of the ideas of the people it conquered. These people were also able to go on **worshipping** their own gods and keep their own customs. The Romans also slowly granted **citizenship** to conquered people. They governed a **multicultural** empire.

Freedom of religion is an example of multiculturalism in many modern countries. Here, You can see a Christian church (right) close to a Muslim mosque (left) in St Petersburg, Russia.

ПЕТРОВСКАЯ
набережная

...NOW

Many countries today are a mix of people from different places and cultures. Modern governments face the challenge of making laws that are fair to all their people. Like the Romans, they can take the good from different cultures and make it part of their own.

Who were the Roman soldiers and gladiators?

Without the Roman army, there would have been no Roman **Empire**. Soldiers were called **legionaries**. They were tough and well trained. Legionaries served for 20 years. The Roman army was divided into divisions, called legions, of about 5,000 men. Legions were made up of smaller units called centuries. These had around 80 men, controlled by a commander. The Roman army also had soldiers who fought on horseback, as well as those who fought with bows and arrows.

The army

Young men from wealthy families often joined the army as a first step towards a political career. For the poor, joining the army was a way to earn money, land, and **citizenship**. When they retired, many soldiers settled down and raised families in the distant lands where they had fought. They helped spread the Latin language and Roman culture throughout the empire.

Tough soldiers

Each Roman soldier carried about 30 kilograms (70 pounds) of gear when they marched!

THEN...

There was more to the Roman army than just fighting. Soldiers also built roads, bridges, town walls, harbours, and **aqueducts**. The army also acted as a police force throughout the empire. They maintained law and order and protected trade.

The Roman army did a lot of building as well as fighting. Modern armies have groups who are experts at building things like bridges very quickly, as this photograph shows.

...NOW

Armies today often help to build and maintain roads, bridges, and dams. Sometimes, they even help build schools, hospitals, and other public projects in parts of the world where they are needed.

Celebrating victory

The Romans celebrated their military victories in style. Soldiers who had fought hard battles came home to march in parades through the city. Special arches and columns were built to honour great battles and generals. Julius Caesar is the most famous Roman general. His victories allowed him to take control of Rome.

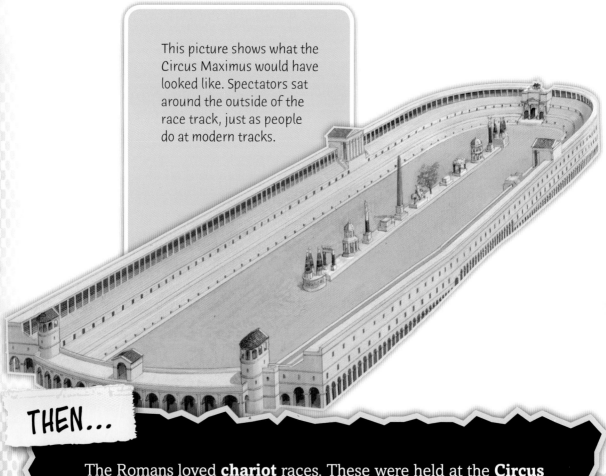

This picture shows what the Circus Maximus would have looked like. Spectators sat around the outside of the race track, just as people do at modern tracks.

THEN...

The Romans loved **chariot** races. These were held at the **Circus Maximus**. Charioteers often crashed, or were thrown from their chariots and trampled by their horses. Some charioteers survived long enough to become famous. A man named Gaius Appuleius Diocles won 1,462 races and retired a wealthy man.

Gladiators

Legionaries were not the only type of warrior in Rome. There were also gladiators who fought in front of audiences in **amphitheatres**. Gladiators were usually prisoners taken in war, slaves, or criminals. They fought each other as well as wild animals, and the fights were often to the death. Some were given back their freedom after great performances.

Woman gladiators

Women sometimes fought as gladiators in Rome. They were called gladiatrix.

Boxers are like modern-day gladiators. Some can win fame and fortune.

...NOW

Some of today's sports are still very violent, although athletes no longer fight to the death! Boxing and wrestling are still popular, and car racing is both exciting and dangerous. Muhammad Ali was a boxer in modern times, and he is still one of the most famous sportsmen in history.

What did the Romans know about medicine and science?

Rome was always at war, so healers became very good at treating injuries. They knew that wounds needed to be cleaned to prevent infections. They used wine and vinegar as **antiseptics**. Healers had tools made of metal and could perform operations.

Galen was a famous Roman healer. He used the knowledge of the ancient Greeks in his work and added his own theories. Galen studied the human body, but because dissecting (cutting up) dead human bodies was not allowed in Rome, he used pig and monkey bodies instead. His work influenced healers and doctors for many centuries.

The codex

The Romans invented the modern form of the book, called a **codex**. It replaced scrolls, which were rolls of paper. The codex allowed more information to be written in a smaller area.

THEN...

The Roman language, Latin, spread all over the **empire**. It was spoken for hundreds of years. Today, it is no longer spoken, and because of this it is often called a dead language. However, many modern languages such as French, Italian, Spanish, and Portuguese come from Latin.

This photograph shows an open codex from the Middle Ages. Unlike in modern paper books, codex pages were made from a thin leather, called vellum. Some of the knowledge of Roman scholars has survived because it was written down in codexes.

...NOW

Latin is still used in medicine, science, the law, religious texts, and even in some expressions we use every day. When telling time, for example, "a.m." is short for *ante meridiem*, which means "before noon", and "p.m." is short for *post meridiem*, or "after noon".

The calendar and other inventions

Julius Caesar used the advice of **astronomers** to create the Julian calendar. This calendar was used for hundreds of years and many of the names of our months come from Roman times. For example, January was named for the god of new beginnings Janus, and March for the god of war Mars. July is named for Julius Caesar, and August for the Emperor Augustus.

The ancient Romans invented the odometer. An odometer is an instrument used to measure distances travelled. The Romans invented shoes of different shapes to fit the right and left foot – something we take for granted today! The Romans also invented indoor plumbing, sewer systems, and heated baths.

In a hypocaust system, the floor was raised above the ground by pillars. Hot air then moved around this space, heating the room above.

THEN...

The ancient Romans built large public baths. Some Roman baths were built on natural hot springs that were used to heat the water. When they didn't have a natural hot spring, the Romans used something they invented called a **hypocaust**. In a hypocaust system, the Romans used a furnace to create hot air. The hot air then passed through a space beneath the pools, heating the water above. Romans also used hypocausts to heat houses.

Ambient heating first heats the floors. The heat then rises and warms the air inside the room or building.

...NOW

Today, we call the Roman way of heating pools and rooms by pumping heated air under the floors ambient heating. This type of heating is becoming popular again because it is **efficient** and healthy. Modern ambient heating can be created using electricity. It can also still be created using hot water, as the Romans did it.

What was Roman art and architecture like?

The Romans created many works of art, including sculptures, **mosaics**, and **frescoes**. Public buildings and the homes of the wealthy were often painted with colourful frescoes and the floors were covered with mosaics.

Glass-blowing was a Roman invention. Using this method, items made from glass were easy to produce and became as common as pottery. Glass was used for drinking out of, just as it is still used today.

This illustration shows what the Colosseum would have looked like in Roman times, with its many arches and grand statues.

THEN...

The Colosseum in Rome is made of concrete, stone, and white marble. There are 80 arched entrances, and it held an audience of 50,000 people. A canvas could be raised above the seats to shield people from the sun and rain. The **Circus Maximus** could hold a crowd of 250,000 people.

Car racing events can draw a huge crowd of as many as 150,000 people to watch the dangerous, high-speed races. That's a huge crowd, but not as big as the **chariot** race crowds at the Circus Maximus.

...NOW

Modern stadiums are not so very different from the Colosseum. Some have covers that can open and close to protect the audience from sun and rain, just like in Roman times. Today, the thousands of excited fans watching car racing or football matches experience a similar thrill to the crowds at the Colosseum or Circus Maximus in ancient Rome.

Concrete

Many Roman buildings and structures are still standing. The Romans invented the arch, which allowed structures to support a lot of weight. **Aqueducts** used arches to carry fresh water into cities. The invention of concrete allowed the Romans to create domed structures like the Pantheon. The Pantheon is still standing after more than 1,800 years.

To make concrete, the Romans mixed volcanic ash, limestone, sand, and water. This concrete could be used underwater, which was helpful for making bridges. The aqueducts, sewers, and buildings of Rome would not have been possible without the invention of concrete. Today, concrete is still a useful and common building material found all over the world.

Milestones

Milestones were a Roman invention. They were stones placed alongside roads to mark distances. We have road signs that do the same thing today.

THEN...

Over time, the ancient Romans built thousands of kilometres of roads. All the roads started in Rome and connected it to the farthest reaches of the **empire**. This meant that messengers and armies could travel quickly. The roads also allowed for safer trade between different parts of the empire. The Romans designed roads to be higher in the middle so that rainwater would run down into drainage ditches along the sides.

The Romans built things to last. Aqueducts, such as this one in France, are still standing in many places around the former Roman Empire.

...NOW

The Appian Way of ancient Rome could be considered the first motorway. In modern times, large motorways connect most cities and towns. Motorways have made long-distance travel and trade over land much easier and worthwhile. Post, goods, and people can move great distances on motorways using modern high-speed vehicles.

Key dates

Here is an outline of some important moments in the history and culture of ancient Rome:

753 BC	Rome is founded
around 600 BC	Earliest evidence of Latin writing
500s BC	Temples are built
509 BC	The Roman Republic is founded
450 BC	First Roman law codes are made
329 BC	The **Circus Maximus** is built in Rome. It is rebuilt and expanded over several centuries.
312 BC	The Appian Way (an important Roman road) and the first Roman **aqueduct**, the Aqua Appia, are built
around 280 BC	Earliest evidence of Roman coins
272 BC	Rome wins control of all of Italy
264 BC	First gladiatorial games are held
200s BC	First use of the **codex**
206 BC	Spain becomes two Roman provinces
146 BC	North Africa becomes a Roman province

46 BC	Julius Caesar becomes the first dictator of Rome. He introduces the Julian calendar.
44 BC	Julius Caesar is assassinated
27 BC	Octavian becomes Augustus, the first Roman emperor. This marks the beginning of the Roman **Empire**.
AD 43	Rome conquers Britain
AD 64	Fire nearly destroys Rome
AD 64	First persecution of Christians
AD 70–80	The Colosseum is built in Rome
AD 118–125	The Emperor Hadrian builds the Pantheon
AD 212	Roman **citizenship** is given to all free people in the Roman Empire
AD 306	Constantine becomes the first Christian emperor
AD 476	The last Roman emperor, Romulus Augustus, is defeated by Odoacer, a **Gothic** general

Glossary

AD short for Anno Domini, which is Latin for "in the year of our Lord". AD is used for all the years after year 1.

amphitheatre large circular building with many rows of seats, very similar to modern-day stadiums

antiseptic substance put on a wound to stop it getting infected

appeal request to a court or legal authority, asking for a decision to be changed

aqueduct bridge-like structure that carries water

astronomer person who studies the stars and planets

BC short for before Christ. BC is used for all the years before year 1.

chariot two-wheeled vehicle drawn by horses, used in Roman wars and races

Circus Maximus the largest chariot racing stadium in Rome. It was also used for other sporting entertainment.

citizenship legal right of belonging to a country

codex ancient book, similar to a modern book, written by hand

efficient works well without wasting time, money, or energy

empire large territory governed by a powerful ruler

fresco painting made on a wall while the plaster is still wet

glass-blowing art of forming glass into a particular shape by blowing air into it through a tube while it is softened by heat

Gothic belonging to a tribe of people from an area that is now Germany

hypocaust space under the floor of an ancient Roman building where heat passed through from a furnace to heat the room or bath

impartial fair, just, and not favouring one side or the other

jury group of people sworn to give a verdict (decision) to a court on a legal question

Justinian Code set of Roman laws compiled under Emperor Justinian I in order to create a simple and clear system of laws for the entire Roman Empire

legend ancient story which is not necessarily based on facts

legionary name for a Roman soldier who was a member of a group called a legion

mosaic picture or design made of small, coloured pieces of tile, stone, or glass, fitted together

multicultural made up of people from many different cultures, who live in the same area

patrician person belonging to the upper class who governed in ancient Rome

plebeian ordinary person who had no special power in ancient Rome

strigil curved blade used to scrape away sweat and dirt from the skin

superstition fear of the unknown or mysterious that is not based on knowledge or reason

toga robe worn by Roman men who were citizens

tunic long, loose piece of clothing worn by most people in Rome, sometimes with a belt

worship praising and showing respect for a god or gods. It may involve singing, praying, and other ways of showing respect.

Find out more

Books

Ancient Rome, Simon James (Dorling Kindersley, 2008)

History from Objects: The Romans, John Malam (Wayland, 2010)

The Roman Colosseum, Fiona MacDonald (Book House, 2010)

Websites

www.rome.mrdonn.org
This website has lots of information on the history and everyday life of the ancient Romans.

www.historyforkids.org/learn/romans
Find out about ancient Roman clothes, art, science, and much more on this useful website.

Index